WESTERN STEAM IN COLOUR
Hugh Ballantyne

First published 1983 by Jane's Publishing Company Ltd
This edition published 1990 by Ian Allan Ltd

ISBN 0 7110 1883 9

Published by

IAN ALLAN LTD

Terminal House Shepperton TW17 8AS
Telephone: Walton-on-Thames (0932) 228950
Fax: 0932 232366   Telex: 929806 IALLAN G
Registered Office: Terminal House Shepperton TW17 8AS
Printed by Ian Allan Printing Ltd at their works at Coombelands
in Runnymede, England

Cover illustrations

Front: the Western Region at its best, continuing the fine tradition of
the GWR, a gleaming Brunswick green locomotive with polished brass
and copper shining in the sun, hauling chocolate and cream stock.
'Castle' No 7035 *Ogmore Castle* approaching Purton before the steady
climb to Sapperton with the down 'Cheltenham Spa Express', 5.00 pm
Paddington to Cheltenham St James. 18 June 1962. (*Hugh Ballantyne*)
Voigtlander CLR

Back: morning preparation at Wolverhampton Stafford Road shed. 24
August 1963. (*Hugh Ballantyne*)
Voigtlander CLR   Agfa CT18

Right: this picture is a reminder of just how labour intensive the
railways were in the steam era and that the work was often hard and
totally unglamorous. Old Oak Common 'Castle' class No 5010
Restormel Castle rests under the coaling stage at Llandore shed, no
doubt between a spell of duty on express working before returning
from Swansea to London, as a shed man laboriously tips a tub of coal
into the 'Castle's' tender. This engine was one of the earliest 'Castle'
class to be withdrawn, suffering its fate as long ago as December 1959.
4 January 1959. (*Peter W Gray*)
Voigtlander Vito IIa   Agfa CT18   1/125, f8

Introduction

With the GWR's gas-turbine experiment not proven and main line diesel traction in its infancy, steam reigned supreme on the Western Region in the mid-1950s. Swindon and other workshops reverted to turning out even mixed traffic locomotives in lined green livery, brown and cream stock re-appeared on principal expresses and with the introduction of notable services like 'The Bristolian', pre-war standards of train running were restored. Nationalisation and austerity had not crushed the GWR spirit and it was very much business as before at Swindon and Paddington.

To its many devotees the GWR, and later the Western, was different. The railway was operated by a distinctive family of locomotives, development of which was unhindered by the Grouping. While standardised designs of rolling stock, structures and signalling also contributed greatly to the unique quality of the system, the picture was undoubtedly completed by Swindon's magnificent locomotives. Certainly the LMS and Standard designs introduced to the WR in the 1950s appeared to the casual observer slightly out of place, irrespective of their value to the operating department although green paint, where applied, helped a little!

In 1955, however, BR was to announce a programme of traction modernisation which, over the course of the next ten years, would dismantle the entire apparatus of Western steam as the region became the first to fall to diesel traction in 1965. Still worse was to follow in 1963 when Beeching unveiled his plans to prune unremunerative lines and services, spelling doom for many parts of the WR network.

Fortunately this twilight of BR steam and the final days of so many of our country's rural branch lines and secondary routes coincided with a steady improvement in the quality of colour film and photographic equipment, as well as a general rise in living standards. Although this bore no comparison to today's materials, equipment and affluence, not least the huge array of instantly available lenses and fast colour films to suit all needs, this improvement gradually allowed the photographers of the era more freedom to pursue their quarry and form a lasting and colourful record of this key period in British railway history.

In selecting the pictures for this album I have sought to bring together a good selection of the main GWR locomotive types which saw BR service as well as a few of the later Standard designs which were either built at Swindon or found a home on the region. At the same time an attempt has been made to portray a wide range of Western steam activity in many parts of the Great Western empire, truly a geographically varied system. The pleasant task of assembling these photographs has evoked many memories of the outstanding and distinctive qualities of the Western and the beautiful country which it served so well. I have spent many happy days on journeys or holidays from my native Bath, deep in Great Western territory, travelling on or photographing the system, and I hope these pictures will bring back similar memories to readers.

The author and publishers are much indebted to the photographers who have so kindly made available their literally invaluable and quite irreplaceable transparencies from their collections for this book. Their important contribution has allowed me much greater freedom to portray some of the many facets of one of the world's great railway systems.

HUGH BALLANTYNE
Eccleshall, North Staffordshire
June 1983

Opposite. Prior to the collapse of two of the spans of the Severn Bridge due to barge collision in October 1960, Sharpness was the main intermediate station on the east bank of the Severn of the former Severn & Wye Joint Railway operated by the GWR and Midland companies. This picture shows the Midland influence in the style of station building and nameboard, whilst the train is pure Great Western. Collett 0-4-2T No 1409, in unlined green livery, stands with auto coach W1668W in the much diminished and forlorn station on arrival as the 4.55 pm from Berkeley Road. 20 July 1963. (*Hugh Ballantyne*)
Voigtlander CLR   Agfa CT18   f8, 1/60

Above. Between Saunderton and Princes Risborough, on the former GW & LNE Joint line which gave the GWR its shorter route to Birmingham, the up and down lines diverge on different elevations at the summit over the Chilterns on the 350 feet contour. 'King' class No 6019 *King Henry V* has just come over the summit and will drop down at 1 in 88 to Princes Risborough before reaching the undulating section of line onwards to Banbury and beyond

with the 9.10 am Paddington to Birkenhead. 25 August 1962. *(Peter A Fry)*
Kodak Retinette 1B   Agfa CT18

Opposite. The last of the thirty 'Kings', immaculately turned out No 6029 *King Edward VIII*, built in 1930 and called *King Stephen* until 1936, comes to a halt at Solihull with the 3.10 pm Paddington to Wolverhampton Low Level.

This was one of the additional London, Birmingham and Wolverhampton workings introduced on the former GWR route at the start of the 1959 winter timetable when most of the former LMS line trains to these cities were withdrawn during preparations for electrification of the line from Euston. 9 May 1961. *(Michael Mensing)*
Hasselblad 1000F   Agfa CT18
f4.5, 1/250

Now entirely devoid of railways, Tavistock, situated on the western fringe of Dartmoor and birthplace of Sir Francis Drake, once had two stations as it was served by both the GWR and the London & South Western Railway. The Great Western station, originally built in 1859 complete with overall roof for the broad gauge South Devon Railway, was still in existence over one hundred years later, as seen here. During BR days the station became known as Tavistock South and was the principle station on the branch from Marsh Mills, Tavistock Junction, to Launceston, a distance of 31¾ miles. On a pleasant summer evening, 4575 class 2–6–2T No 5569 pauses with the 5.50 pm Launceston to Plymouth train. 8 August 1961. (*Hugh Ballantyne*)

Voigtlander CLR   Agfa CT18   f5.6, 1/60

A picture which epitomises how well the GWR blended into – and served – so much of England's green and pleasant land. This pastoral scene shows the simple but functional terminus layout at Kingsbridge, a small town lying in the South Hams region of South Devon. It was the end of a 12¾ mile long branch from Brent, where connection was made with the main Exeter to Plymouth line. Churchward-designed small Prairie tank No 4561 basks in the afternoon sunshine before taking the 4.00 pm train northwards to Brent. 8 June 1961. (*Peter W Gray*)
Agfa Super Silette   Kodachrome I   f4, 1/60

On a warm evening in mid-summer 'Grange' class No 6833 *Calcot Grange* approaches Bath Spa station with the 5.35 pm Salisbury to Cardiff train, against the backcloth of elegant Georgian and Regency houses built in the local limestone on the slopes of Bathwick Hill. 29 June 1961. (*Hugh Ballantyne*)

Voigtlander CLR   *Agfa CT18*   *f2.8, 1/250*

Canton, principal locomotive shed in Cardiff had a fine reputation for turning out many of its passenger locomotives in immaculate condition. The shed closed to steam in September 1962 but its remaining steam jobs transferred to Cardiff East Dock shed, until their gradual replacement by diesels was effected. The standard of turnout continued at East Dock and its efforts are seen here by the spotless condition of 'Hall' class No 6944 *Fledborough Hall*, positively gleaming in the evening sunlight as it sets out from Bath Spa station with the 5.25 pm Salisbury to Cardiff train. An unusual feature at Bath was the position of the station signal box, which can be seen situated over the roof of the down platform. 30 April 1963. (*Hugh Ballantyne*)

Voigtlander CLR   Perutz C18   f4, 1/125

Above. Scene in the shed yard at Cardiff's principal shed, Canton, situated in the fork of the lines to Neath and Barry just west of Cardiff General station. At the time of nationalisation in 1948 it had an allocation of 122 engines. It was opened in 1861 and was closed to steam 101 years later in September 1962. In this picture the shed is still busy and being prepared or cleaned in its smoky atmosphere are (left to right): No 7820 *Dinmore Manor*, No 5984 *Linden Hall* and No 5961 *Toynbee Hall*. 12 November 1961. (*Hugh Ballantyne*)
Voigtlander CLR   Perutz C18   f8, 1/30

Opposite. One of the BR-built 'Castles', No 7022 *Hereford Castle* simmers gently outside Swindon shed whilst acting as the Swindon stand-by loco for the interesting grand finale of GWR express running, the high speed run back to Paddington from Bristol by sister engine 5054. This event was organised by Ian Allan Ltd in conjunction with the Western Region and comprised a Paddington–Plymouth–Bristol–Paddington round trip using three 'Castles' working on very fast timings. It was a gallant effort, sadly marred by the failure of 4079 near Westbury on the first leg, but with brilliant deputising by No 6991

Capel Dewi Hall to Taunton. On the final stage 5054 managed 94 mph near Little Somerford, just short of the 'ton' hoped for. If this was not enough excitement for one day, the RCTS brought a distinguished visitor to Swindon, partly seen here, in the shape of 'Coronation' class No 46251 *City of Nottingham* with the 'East Midland Rail Tour' from Nottingham. 9 May 1964. (*Hugh Ballantyne*)
Voigtlander CLR   Agfa CT18   f8, 1/60

Above. Keynsham is the home of a major chocolate factory once owned by J S Fry & Son Ltd, whose products were a household name until the company name disappeared into the Cadbury-Schweppes conglomerate, and a siding of over half a mile in length was provided to carry rail-borne goods out of the factory. Connection with the GWR was at the east end of the station up platform and at one time traffic was such that two trains a day worked in and out of the siding. This duty was for some years performed by the Great Western's antique acquisitions from the Weston, Clevedon & Portishead Railway in 1940, the two Brighton 'Terriers', which became GWR No 5 *Portishead* and No 6, but after their demise Pannier tanks took over. By the time this photograph was taken traffic was reduced to one train per day, and indeed steam was nearly finished in this area, as seen by the work weary condition of No 9623. The engine and brake van are coming out of the chocolate factory and crossing the A4175 Willsbridge road before regaining Western metals. 8 October 1964 (*Russell Leitch*)

Opposite. Avoncliff Halt, just west of Bradford on Avon in Wiltshire, is still open for passenger trains, but in this scene 5700 class 0–6–0PT No 3632 hurries towards Bath and Bristol with a light goods train from Westbury. 22 September 1962. (*Peter A Fry*)
Kodak Retinette IB   *Agfa CT18*

The 'Chalford Flyer' was the name given by the local people to one celebrated example of that well known institution much beloved by the Great Western, a push-pull auto train service. This one ran between Gloucester Central and Chalford, the latter station situated on the main line to Swindon sixteen miles from Gloucester at the eastern end of the Golden valley, although the principle station served by these trains was Stroud. In this view of the Golden Valley looking towards Stroud, partly visible in the distance, the little 0–4–2T No 1458 is pushing its two auto trailers towards the small platforms of Ham Mill Halt as it works the 12.30 pm Chalford to Gloucester Central service. In this journey there were ten stops in the seven miles to Stonehouse followed by a gallop of nine miles northwards to Gloucester, most of which took place with the parallel Midland line alongside. 10 October 1964. (*Hugh Ballantyne*)

Voigtlander CLR   *Agfa CT18*   *f5.6, 1/250*

Seen here at Stroud is 1400 class 0–4–2T No 1453 drawing out with the 2.10 pm auto train from Gloucester with 4¼ miles to go and six more stops to make. On the left, large Collett Prairie No 6128 waits on the down line to cross over to the up when No 1453 has cleared the section to return to Brimscombe, its base, to await its next call for duty banking trains up to Sapperton. 10 October 1964. (*Hugh Ballantyne*)
Voigtlander CLR   Agfa CT18   f5.6, 1/250

Portrait of the prototype 4–6–0 'County', No 1000 *County of Middlesex*, which could be regarded as the final development of the 'Saint', keeping within the 20-ton axle load limit. Mr Hawksworth introduced a number of new features, including a new Standard No 15 boiler with 280 lbs pressure, the highest on a GWR locomotive. The coupled wheels of 6 ft 3 in were not standard and the continuous splasher and straight nameplates were new departures. No 1000 is seen here with the experimental double chimney originally fitted, but this was not as efficient as hoped for because the effect of the blast was not proportional to the steam requirements, tending to pull the fire to pieces when the engine was being worked hard. Consequently, this locomotive in 1958 was fitted with the short elliptical double chimney eventually fitted to all the class. 5 May 1956. (*R C Riley*) *Agfa Silette f3.5 lens   Kodachrome 8ASA f4, 1/60*

On a beautiful St George's Day, high up in the Cotswolds near the village of Coates and the source of the River Thames, 'County' class No 1010 *County of Caernarvon* drifts over the summit from Sapperton down to the stop at Kemble with the 2.30 pm Cheltenham St James to Paddington train. 23 April 1962. (*Hugh Ballantyne*)

Voigtlander CLR   *Agfa CT18*   *f5.6, 1/250*

Above. A fine action picture of a 'Castle' at work on an express train. Appropriately it is No 7007 *Great Western*, so named in January 1948 to commemorate the fact that this engine was the last express passenger locomotive built by the company. Originally named *Ogmore Castle*, it was completed at Swindon in July 1946 and was subsequently fitted with a double chimney in 1961, one of 66 'Castles' so treated. Here she is going well on the down fast line near Iver with the 5.15 pm Paddington to Hereford, the 'Cathedrals Express'. 25 August 1962. (*Peter A Fry*)
Kodak Retinette IB   Agfa CT18

Opposite. Nocturnal activity at Newton Abbot with the splendid sight of a double-headed 'Castle' hauled train ready for departure. No 4087 *Cardigan Castle* is piloting No 7022 *Hereford Castle* on a return football excursion from Plymouth to Broxbourne. On the extreme left 'Hall' No 4991 *Cobham Hall* has charge of the 7.30 pm Newton Abbot to Taunton parcels train. 27 January 1962. (*Peter W Gray*)
Agfa Super Silette   Kodachrome II
f2, 30 secs

Above. The Churward 4300 class, comprising 342 engines built between 1911 and 1932, was a versatile mixed traffic engine to be found over most of the GWR system. Taunton's allocation usually consisted of about nine, mainly for use on the Barnstaple and Minehead lines. In this scene a work stained No 5336, built in 1917 and then the oldest class survivor, has just been turned on Barnstaple Junction's turntable prior to working home to Taunton on the next passenger train. 29 February 1964. (*Hugh Ballantyne*)
Voigtlander CLR   Agfa CT18   f8, 1/60

Opposite. As late afternoon shadows lengthen in the industrial West Midlands, 4300 class 2–6–0 No 6319 draws a train of ECS off the Wombourn line at Kingswinford Junction, just north of Brettell Lane on the Stourbridge Junction to Wolverhampton line. 26 August 1961. (*Michael Mensing*)
Hasselblad 1000F   High Speed Ektachrome f4.5, 1/500

Above. Other than the solitary Pacific No 111 *The Great Bear*, Churchward's largest locomotive design was a small batch of handsome mixed traffic 2–8–0s, class 4700, the first of which appeared in 1919. No 4700 was rebuilt with a larger standard No 7 boiler in 1921 and then it was followed by eight more similar engines in 1922 & 1923. The locos had 5 ft 8 in coupled wheels and although originally put to work on night express goods trains, they became used on other fitted goods and, latterly, summer express passenger services between London and the West of England. Most of them spent their lives allocated to Old Oak Common and appro-

priately this picture shows No 4705, built in 1923, (with another 4700 behind) in sparkling condition at that shed. In forty years of service this engine amassed the highest mileage for the class, over 1,656,000 miles. May 1960. (*Basil Roberts*)

Kodak Retinette IB   Agfa CT18

Opposite. Sweeping down the valley of the River Kennet near Hungerford on a summer day, the big Churchward mixed traffic 2–8–0 No 4706 is going fast with the Saturday 1.25 pm Padding-

ton to Kingswear express. This part of the main line to Plymouth, incongruously known as the Berks & Hants line, stemmed from the fact that the original lines from Reading went south to Basingstoke and westwards to Hungerford from Southcote Junction. After the opening of the direct line to Taunton with its various cut-offs, this route took all the through Devon and Cornwall traffic from London, but the old name, used in conjunction with the still important connecting line to Basingstoke, stuck. 4 July 1959. (*R C Riley*)

Agfa Super Silette   f2 Solagon
Kodachrome 8 ASA   f2.5, 1/250

Left. A view of the interior of Worcester locomotive works showing three engines under repair. Front to rear: No 5932 *Haydon Hall*, 5700 class No 3683 and 'Castle' class No 5042 *Winchester Castle*. This picture shows just how limited space was in the workshop, as the 'Castle' and 'Hall' cannot entirely be fitted inside, the cabs overhanging the front doors of their respective bays. The works closed in November 1965 and the buildings have since been demolished. 12 July 1964. (*Hugh Ballantyne*)

Voigtlander CLR   *Agfa CT18*   *f2.8 1/30*

Above. Clear evidence from this picture that the 'Halls' were designed as mixed traffic engines is shown by No 5945 *Leckhampton Hall* coming to the end of its 1 in 100 uphill slog from the Severn Tunnel at Patchway with a Severn Tunnel Junction to Stoke Gifford goods train on a cold March morning. 17 March 1962. (*Hugh Ballantyne*)

Voigtlander CLR   *Perutz C18*   *f5.6, 1/250*

In 1931 Mr Collett introduced the 6100 class, another series of large Prairie tank, and very similar to his 5101 class except for the slightly higher boiler pressure of 225 lbs. Seventy were built between 1931 and 1935 and were put to work in the London Division on improved London suburban services. Generally most of the class remained in the area including No 6132, seen standing outside the carriage shed at Old Oak Common during a spell of duty as one of the stock pilots. Despite DMUs taking over the London local services in 1960 some of the class survived the onslaught and were transferred to other duties: 31 of the class remained until 1965, twelve right until the end of Western Region steam in December of that year. This engine was withdrawn in October 1965. May 1960. (*Basil Roberts*)
Kodak Retinette IB

A study of a Churchward express locomotive, 'Star' class 4–6–0 No 4056 *Princess Margaret*, seen standing in the shed yard at Old Oak Common. After tests with three French compound Atlantics bought for the purpose, Mr Churchward designed a 4-cylinder simple engine with long valve travel on his already proven Standard No 1 boiler. The result was No 40 *North Star*, the first of what was to become the 'Star' class, one of the most free running 4–6–0s ever built, and the outstanding British express locomotive design of the period. Not surprisingly, this remained the basis for all the larger GWR express passenger engines through to the 'Castles' and 'Kings'. No 4000 appeared as a 4–4–2 in 1906 and after comparative tests with the French Atlantics was converted to a 4–6–0 in 1909. The remaining 72 'Stars' were built as 4–6–0s in seven batches between 1907 and 1923, this particular engine being in the fifteen emerging from Swindon during 1914, all of which carried names of Princesses. No 4056 was fitted with elbow outside steam pipes in 1949 and this is clearly visible in the picture. It was the last of the class to be withdrawn in October 1957 and amassed the highest class mileage of over two million miles. In the background can be seen another interesting locomotive, the prototype 'Hall' No 4900 *Saint Martin*. 23 September 1956. (*R C Riley*)
Agfa Silette   f3.5 lens
Kodachrome 8 ASA   f2.8, 1/125

Above. A busy scene at Yatton on a summer Saturday. 'Hall' class No 6957 *Norcliffe Hall* is drawing into the platform with the Saturdays only 9.40 am Carmarthen to Weston-super-Mare train. As proclaimed on the large station nameboard, on the right is 0–6–0PT No 3702 waiting with the 2.45 pm train to Cheddar and Witham and, on the left, a single unit railcar working as the 2.40 pm to Clevedon, a small Somerset seaside resort 3½ miles away. 17 August 1963. (*Hugh Ballantyne*)
Voigtlander CLR   Agfa CT18   f8, 1/125

Opposite. A picture recapturing the scene which prevailed for many years at Weymouth Quay. The GWR developed a heavy flow of traffic to and from the Channel Islands via Weymouth, and to get to the quayside trains traversed a line laid through the streets of the town for a mile. Motive power for all the trains over this section was for a long time provided by a small Collett-designed outside cylinder class 1366 0–6–0PTs, six of which were built in 1934. One of these attractive little engines stands on the quay with the Great Western's steamer *St Helier* adjacent. This ship and its sister the *St Julien* were a pair of turbine steamers built by John Brown of Clydebank for the GWR in 1925 both having a displacement of 1885 tons and a speed of 18 knots. The *St Helier* had a very distinguished career, not only taking part in the 1940 Dunkirk evacuation but in the Normandy landings of 1944 as well. After the war she was the vessel which reopened the Channel Islands service in June 1946. Her last voyage was on 14 September 1960 and she was subsequently scrapped. Likewise No 1370 was withdrawn that year, in January, her job being taken over by 204 hp diesel shunters. Fortunately one of the class, No 1369, is preserved at Buckfastleigh on the Dart Valley Railway. 24 July 1958. (*R C Riley*)
Agfa Super Silette   f2 Solagon
Kodachrome 8 ASA   f3.5, 1/125

Left. A fine view from the up 'Royal Duchy', 11.05 am Penzance–Paddington, as 'Grange' class No 6832 *Brockton Grange* takes the train onto the single line over Brunel's masterpiece, the Royal Albert Bridge at Saltash, which spans the River Tamar and marks the boundary between Cornwall and Devon. 29 September 1959. (*Peter W Gray*)
Agfa Super Silette   Kodachrome II f3.5, 1/250

Above. From this view taken over 25 years ago at the west end of the up platform of Truro station, looking east, the appearance of the station is little changed today. Even the bay platform on the right is still used by Falmouth trains, albeit DMU-worked rather than by the loco-hauled non-corridor stock used when the photograph was taken. Here No 4992 *Crosby Hall* starts the down 'Cornishman', 9.00 am Wolverhampton to Penzance, out of Cornwall's capital city with

three more stops before reaching the end of the line at Penzance. 24 July 1957. (*Peter W Gray*)
Voigtlander Vito IIa   Kodachrome I f4.5, 1/15

A scene inside 'A' shop, the great main erecting shop at Swindon Works, showing the superb way in which all GWR locomotives were treated upon overhaul. The quality of repair and standard of finish applied to the locomotives passing through the Works was unsurpassed anywhere in the world, and the evidence of the finished product is shown here. Even as late in the history of British steam as 1963, Swindon continued to maintain its impeccable standards. The three engines shown here in the bays down the east side of 'A' Shop are (left to right): 2-6-2T No 4160, 'Modified Hall' No 7907 *Hart Hall*, 0-6-0 No 3218 and the Collett style cab of 2884 class 2-8-0 No 3850. 28 July 1963. (*Hugh Ballantyne*)
Voigtlander CLR   Agfa CT18   f4, 1/15

All engines ex-works at Swindon were turned out to the highest standards both mechanically and visually. This low angle view of 7200 class 2-8-2T No 7253, one of the GWR's largest tank engines, shows that this excellent finish applied equally to heavy goods engines besides passenger locomotives. The 7200 class were Collett rebuilds of earlier Churchward 2-8-0Ts effected by extending their frames to accommodate a trailing radial axle and larger bunker, so increasing their fuel capacity and widening their range of work. This engine was the last of the class, being rebuilt from No 4245 in December 1939. 14 October 1962. (*Peter W Gray*)
Agfa Super Silette   Kodachrome II f8, 1/60

A picture which illustrates the work to which the Collett heavy duty 7200 class 2–8–2Ts were put and so competently performed. Their main use was medium or long distance coal trains and for this reason the majority of them were allocated to South Wales sheds. People such as the photographer, who lived near the main Bristol line, had the opportunity to see them on the regular duty of hauling heavily laden coal trains en route from South Wales via Bath and Salisbury to the south of England. This scene is typical of such workings, and No 7215 from Ebbw Junction shed, Newport, a regular performer, is seen steadily pulling its heavy load of unfitted wagons on the up line across the long straight embankment of the Somerdale meadows at Keynsham, heading for Salisbury. 2 June 1962. (*Russell Leitch*)

One of the Churchward heavy duty mineral 4200 class 2–8–0Ts, No 4254, resting inside the roundhouse at Bristol St Phillip's Marsh shed. This wheel arrangement was rare for a tank engine and was introduced as a version of the 2800 class 2–8–0 for short distance mineral traffic, such as that found in South Wales. For this reason the class was mainly allocated to and worked in that area and only a few were based at English sheds. 27 October 1963. (*Peter W Gray*)

Agfa Super Silette   Kodachrome II

Above. One of the later Collett series of 2800 known as the 2884 class, No 3820 heads south on the GW lines near Churchdown, between Cheltenham and Gloucester, with a train consisting mainly of bogie bolsters. It is remarkable to reflect that the 2800 class were the first 2-8-0s in the country, Mr Churchward introducing No 2800 (then numbered 97) in 1903 and that the series, only slightly modified from 2884 onwards, served the GWR and Western Region faithfully with upwards of sixty years of hard labour. 16 May 1964. (*Hugh Ballantyne*)
Voigtlander CLR   Agfa CT18   f8, 1/250

Opposite. A sight typical of the era but rarely seen today is a station and goods yard busy, flourishing and full of revenue earning wagon loads. Here at Yeovil Pen Mill station Churchward 2800 class 2-8-0 No 2879 waits for the road with a Swindon to Weymouth goods train, whilst behind in the yard a Southern Railway 'U' class 2-6-0 No 31792 is on a trip working round to Yeovil Town. 31 March 1962. (*Alan Wild*)
Kodak Retinette 1A   Perutz C18   f4, 1/125

Right. In an attractive setting just over the border into Dorset from Somerset, Collett 6400 class 0–6–0PT No 6430 runs gently along the valley of the River Yeo towards Yeovil Town with a shuttle auto train service from Yeovil Junction. The far pair of tracks are the lines from Yeovil Pen Mill to Weymouth. This engine is now preserved on the Dart Valley Railway. 22 August 1964. (*Alan Wild*)
Kodak Retinette 1A   Perutz C18

Opposite. The crew of No 6400 have time for a chat now their train from Plymouth has arrived at its destination of Tavistock. This was the last 6400 class engine to remain at Plymouth when this picture was taken, though once they were allocated in strength to work the Saltash suburban services. The 6400 class 0–6–0PT was a series of forty engines designed by Mr Collett with 4 ft 7½ in coupled wheels for auto train working, and the prototype looks particularly neat seen in its BR style of lined green livery. Partly visible on the right is auto trailer W230W. 8 August 1961. (*Hugh Ballantyne*)
Voigtlander CLR   Agfa CT18
f5.6, 1/60

38

Above. 1963 saw the swansong of the 'Castle' class when most of the remaining members did good work on the Paddington–Worcester–Hereford services. Worcester engines in particular did well, with nine or so Castles at work until official dieselisation of the route in September of that year. Here No 7023 *Penrice Castle* pulls away from Evesham with the 10.05 Hereford to Paddington train. In the foreground is the abandoned track of the Midland branch from Evesham to Broom Junction which was to be lifted in April 1964. 15 April 1963. *(Hugh Ballantyne)*
Voigtlander CLR   Agfa CT18   f5.6, 1/250

Opposite. Kingham was an important rural junction on the main line from Oxford to Worcester with lines going westwards over the Cotswolds to Cheltenham and eastwards to Banbury. Its main line trains ran between London, Worcester and Hereford and in 1962 and before, these were ably powered by 'Castles' and a few 'Halls' from these cities. In this scene, immaculate 'Castle' No 7013 *Bristol Castle* is slowing down to stop briefly whilst en route with the 12.05 pm Hereford to Paddington express. This engine is not all that it appears, as it really is the original No 4082 *Windsor Castle*. These two locomotives exchanged identities in February 1952 when the original No 4082, then under repair in Swindon Works, was required to work the funeral train

for his late Majesty King George VI from Paddington to Windsor. No 7013, being readily available, had No 4082's plates transferred to her. They were never changed back and, to add to the difficulty of identity, the 'new' No 7013 received a double chimney in May 1958 and had its original fluted inside valve casing (the real giveaway to its origin) replaced with a new design of straight type with squared edge to the tread plate and centre portion raised to clear the exhaust passages. As seen here this 1924-built 'Castle' has the appearance of one of the final series, all built after nationalisation. 29 September 1962. *(Hugh Ballantyne)*
Voigtlander CLR   Perutz C18   f4, 1/250

The last new Collett type before his retirement in 1941 was the lightweight 'Manor' class 4–6–0 with a new small Standard No 14 boiler designed to be suitable for running over the GWR's 'blue routes' and so complete the pre-war GWR policy of providing a full range of 4–6–0s for duties covered by passenger tender engines. They always remained a numerically small class, twenty being built in 1938/39 and ten more late in 1950 under Western Region jurisdiction. This portrait shows No 7816 *Frilsham Manor* by the coaling stage at Swindon shed attached to a 3500 gallon tender which, sixteen years after nationalisation, still retains the time honoured initials 'GWR'. The 'Manors' have become a much preserved class, as nineteen of them remained in service to the end of Western steam in 1965, and subsequently nine have been saved from cutting up. 20 September 1964. (*Hugh Ballantyne*)

Voigtlander CLR   Agfa CT18   f8, 1/60

The well known named train serving mid Wales, the 'Cambrian Coast Express' 11.10 am from Paddington to Aberystwyth, made its first stop in Wales at Welshpool. The immaculate 'Manor' No 7823 *Hook Norton Manor* has come onto the train at Shrewsbury for the 81½ mile journey across mid Wales to Aberystwyth. Welshpool station still survives, although the island platform is reduced to one face only and nearly all the goods yard has disappeared. This was once an important railway centre with trains going up the now closed main line of the Cambrian from Buttington Junction to Oswestry and Whitchurch, besides a local all stations service to and from Shrewsbury over what had been the line owned jointly with the LMS. 31 March 1962. *(Hugh Ballantyne)*
Voigtlander CLR   Perutz C18

Above. Getting under way westwards out of Aberystwyth station limits, with the National Library of Wales prominent on the hill in the background, 4300 class No 6384 will take the 5.45 pm train down through a remote part of western Wales to Carmarthen. This involved a journey of 56¼ miles for which 2½ hours were allowed as the train passed by or stopped at 21 intermediate stations or halts. 22 August 1962. (*Peter W Gray*)
Agfa Super Silette   Kodachrome II f3.5, 1/250

Opposite. Pleasant scenery in the heart of mid Wales complemented by the 1 in 52 gradient against east bound trains known as Talerddig bank, between Llanbrynmair and Talerddig on the main Cambrian line, understandably made it a popular place to photograph the action. This picture sums it up very well, not least the fact that one had to contend with dull and wet summer days then, just as now, as Standard class 4 No 75014 works hard to get the 11.25 am Barmouth to Birmingham Snow Hill up to the summit. This engine was one of a class of eighty

all built at Swindon between 1951 and 1954 and has been saved for restoration on the North York Moors Railway. 8 August 1964. (*Peter W Gray*)
Agfa Super Silette   Kodachrome II f2, 1/250

Left. Madeley Junction was once a quiet rural part of Shropshire on the Wolverhampton to Shrewsbury line, as can be seen here with 0–6–0PT No 9639 hauling a coal train on the down line towards Wellington. The junction still exists, and today mgr coal trains diverge off the main line to take coal to Ironbridge power station. However, the location has now changed its appearance following the encroachment of light industrial buildings and new road system caused by the creation of Telford as a new town. 27 August 1962. *(Michael Mensing)*
Hasselblad 1000F   High Speed Ektachrome f6.7, 1/250

Above. The two variations in the 5700 class 0–6–0PTs can be seen in this action picture as one of the later series with larger cab, No 9626, pilots its older sister No 8714, built by Beyer Peacock in 1931, pounding through Clifton Bridge station with a goods train to Portishead. Two features of this part of Bristol are evident in this picture, the tidal River Avon and one of the large brick-built bonded tobacco warehouses, both seen to the left of the train. 17 February 1962. *(Hugh Ballantyne)*
Voigtlander CLR   Perutz C18   f5.6 1/125

The Great Western truly served rural England and that included much of the lovely Devon countryside. The timetable listed two towns called Bampton, one in Oxfordshire on the Fairford branch and this one in north east Devon on the Exe Valley branch to Dulverton. At this station 1400 class 0–4–2T No 1450 pauses at the platform with the 3.25 pm Exeter St Davids to Dulverton train. Sadly this attractive branch was closed in October 1963 but No 1450 remains active in Devon having been safely preserved by the Dart Valley Railway at Buckfastleigh. 28 September 1963. (*Hugh Ballantyne*)

Voigtlander CLR   Agfa CT18   f5.6, 1/60

Crisp autumn sunlight and colours in the trees make for an attractive scene at Hemyock. This was the terminus of a lightly laid 7½ mile branch from Tiverton Junction along the valley of the River Culm in East Devon. Milk from the large dairy was the mainstay traffic, supplemented by three or four weekday passenger trains invariably consisting of a 1400 class engine and one coach. Here is No 1421 having arrived with the 1.42 pm from Tiverton Junction. In the background are some of the six-wheeled tank wagons then extensively used on the many milk trains running from the West of England to the London area. 3 November 1962. (*Peter W Gray*)

Agfa Super Silette   *Kodachrome II*
f4, 1/125

Left. Hawskworth-designed two-cylinder 'County' No 1005 *County of Devon* in the midst of the beautiful rolling green hills of its namesake county toiling slowly up the savage 1 in 44 gradient to the summit at Dainton Tunnel with the 9.05 am Birkenhead to Plymouth train. 5 August 1961. (*Hugh Ballantyne*)
Voigtlander CLR   Agfa CT18   f5.6, 1/250

Above. Despite the apparent beauty of the rolling green fertile South Devon countryside, the railway has to negotiate these hills and valleys between Newton Abbot and Plymouth by means of a continuously curving route with formidable gradients. In this picture 'Hall' class No 4970 *Sketty Hall* is hard at work slogging up the two miles of 1 in 42 from Plympton known as

Hemerdon incline, hauling the 11.20 Plymouth to Taunton train. The stock comprises six coaches in three liveries, old and new BR colours plus the Western Region chocolate and cream used for selected named trains at the time the picture was taken. 8 August 1961. (*Hugh Ballantyne*)
Voigtlander CLR   Agfa CT18   f5.6, 1/250

51

Few people ever contemplate that a beautiful South Devon resort and harbour would handle much commercial traffic, least of all coal, but this remarkable photograph shows just that. The photographer's good local knowledge enabled him to be on hand to capture this scene at Kingswear showing the coaster *Selectivity* discharging coal into the waiting train alongside Kingswear station, with 'Hall' class No 4978 *Westwood Hall* at its head. This was an occasional occurrence and is explained by the fact that the coal train is only making an eight mile journey to the South Western Gas Board's works at Hollacombe, mid-way between Paignton and Torquay. 12 June 1962. *(Peter W Gray)*
Agfa Super Silette   Kodachrome II f4.5, 1/125

On the Kingswear line in South Devon the last six miles from Goodrington Sands Halt were single track with one intermediate station and passing loop at Churston. This was the summit of the single line section and a junction for the short branch down to the fishing village of Brix-ham. Looking east from the road overbridge the photographer has caught one of the earliest 'Castles' built (in 1924) No 4075 *Cardiff Castle* on the 3.05 pm local train from Exeter to Kingswear. Today, this line and Churston station are still open, and GWR engines operated by the Torbay and Dartmouth Railway continue to pass this point. 30 April 1960. (*Peter W Gray*)
Agfa Super Silette   Kodachrome I f2.5, 1/250

Above. The handsome Churchward lines and pedigree are very evident in this picture of the last of the 4500 series 2–6–2Ts with the smaller capacity (1000 gallons) and straight-sided tanks, No 4574, standing inside Plymouth Laira shed. 2 June 1963. (*Rodney A Lissenden*)
Rollicord   Agfa CT18

Opposite. A scene outside the modern shed at Southall, built in 1954 to replace the original 1884 structure on the same site. Collett 4575 class 2–6–2T No 5531 basks in the afternoon sunshine on one of the six roads serving the shed, with two 'Modified Halls', just visible behind. Southall was more readily associated with the large Prairie tanks, not these smaller

'45s' which it only received in 1963 when four of the few survivors were transferred here to work local goods and ballast turns. This engine was withdrawn in December 1964 and the shed lost its steam allocation by August 1965. 8 March 1964. (*Rodney A Lissenden*)
Rollicord   Agfa CT18

Opposite. No 1500, the first of the ten Hawksworth-designed 0–6–0PTs with outside cylinders and short wheelbase, stands with empty stock at Royal Oak outside Paddington. Although a GWR design, these engines were not built until 1949 and represented an unusual departure from the normally neat and tidy appearance of all Great Western engines, being a 'Swindonised' version of the American USATC 0–6–0Ts which the Southern Railway acquired after the war and employed at Southampton Docks. The 1500s mainly found work on ecs trains in and out of Paddington and all had been withdrawn by 1963. Three were sold to the National Coal Board and the one survivor of these, No 1501, is now preserved on the Severn Valley Railway. 19 October 1963. (*R C Riley*)
Agfa Super Silette f2 Solagon
Kodachrome 25ASA   f5.6, 1/125

Left. Not unexpectedly, there is frost on the sleepers during the shortest day of the year when 9400 class 0–6–0PT No 8459's sharp bark reverberates in the still air as she comes around the curve off the Greenford line towards West Ealing on a transfer goods to Acton Yard. 21 December 1963. (*Rodney A Lissenden*)
Rollicord   Agfa CT18

Overleaf

Left. On a lovely late September afternoon Churchward Mogul No 7318 stands at the little wayside platform of Blaisdon Halt, whilst the guard has time for a brief chat with patrons off the 2.25 pm Gloucester Central to Hereford train. Five weeks later the line was closed. 26 September 1964. (*Hugh Ballantyne*)
Voigtlander CLR   Agfa CT18   f8, 1/60

Right. The last day of October 1964 was a golden sunny autumn day, sadly marred by the wretched Beeching 'Axe' striking to close several GWR lines for ever. The Gloucester to Hereford branch, which turned off the main Gloucester to Severn Tunnel Junction at Grange Court Junction, passed through lovely tranquil scenery and, north of Ross-on-Wye, crossed and re-crossed the River Wye as it meandered down the lush countryside. In this picture my wife has beautifully caught the mood of that still autumn day as a Churchward 4300 class Mogul hurries over the placid waters of the River Wye at Backney, in charge of the last 10.25 Hereford to Gloucester train. 31 October 1964. (*Mrs Toni Ballantyne*)
Voigtlander CLR   Agfa CT18   f8, 1/125

Churchward-built 2–8–0 No 2859 has come onto the single line section of the Worcester to Hereford line with a down goods train and is approaching Ledbury Tunnel, which takes the railway under the southern end of the Malvern Hills. The gradient here is 1 in 80 hence the need for the long level refuge siding seen on the left ending in a sand drag as a precaution against runaways. 16 May 1964. (*Michael Mensing*)
Voigtlander Bessa II
High Speed Ektachrome   *f7, 1/250*

Collett 5101 class large Prairie tank No 5152 coming into Ledbury on a cold, crisp Christmas Eve with the 9.15 am Paddington to Hereford train. This engine took over the train at Worcester for the final 29 mile journey and this is its last stop before Hereford. 24 December 1962. (*Peter A Fry*)

Kodak Retinette IB   *Agfa CT18*

Above. A fine action shot of a morning commuter train, the 8.04 am from Lapworth to Birmingham Snow Hill going well behind 5101 class No 4120 between Widney Manor and Solihull. By the time this picture was taken DMUs had been providing the basic service for some years, but during peak hours there were still several regular steam workings. However, all the local non-corridor stock had been withdrawn so the steam trains had to be formed of six or more corridor coaches in an often unsuccessful attempt to bring the seating capacity up to a reasonable level. 9 May 1963. (*Michael Mensing*)
Voigtlander Bessa II
High Speed Ektachrome   *f5, 1/500*

Opposite. The symetrical lines of a Churchward Mogul are well portrayed in this picture, showing the crew at work taking No 7307 out of Acock's Green station with 6.05 pm Birmingham Snow Hill to Leamington Spa. This commuter train was formed out of an earlier working from Stourbridge Junction via Dudley to Birmingham, and was a popular service because it avoided some stops and provided quite a fast train after Solihull and beyond. 27 June 1961. (*Michael Mensing*)
Hasselblad 1000F   *Agfa CT18*
f3.2, 1/500

Above. An unidentified 'Modified Hall' emerges into the afternoon sunshine from Devizes Tunnel and runs into the station of this old Wiltshire market town with the 4.36 pm train from Newbury to Trowbridge. Passengers on this train were compelled to enjoy or suffer a gentle meander through the Berkshire and Wiltshire countryside as this train ambled along, taking two hours to complete its 43 mile journey. 1 June 1963. *(Peter A Fry)*
Kodak Retinette IB   Agfa CT18

Opposite. Activity on the North Warwickshire line at Earlswood Lakes station on a Saturday evening, as 'Modified Hall' No 7915 *Mere Hall*, with its pilot 0–6–0 No 2210 on the inside, arrives with the 11.05 am train from Ilfracombe to Wolverhampton Low Level. The train is stopping to detach the pilot, which in true Great Western practice is coupled inside the train engine. No 2210 has assisted the 'Modified Hall' from Stratford-on-Avon up the steep climb through Wilmcote to the summit here at this station. 25 August 1962. *(Michael Mensing)*
Hasselblad 1000F   High Speed Ektachrome
f4.5, 1/500

Opposite. No 2221, one of the Collett 2251 class, draws into Lechlade station in the evening sunlight with the 4.26 pm train from Oxford to Fairford. Lechlade was the last stop down the line before Fairford on the 21¾ mile East Gloucestershire branch from Yarnton Junction. This end of the line, from Witney to Fairford, was closed to all traffic eight days after this picture was taken, hence the chalked inscription on the smoke-box 'The Fairford Flyer'. This lovely country station subsequently became a coal yard. 8 June 1962. (*Hugh Ballantyne*)
Voigtlander CLR   Perutz C18   f5.6, 1/125

Below. Collett-designed 2251 class 0–6–0 No 3205 and typical GWR signal silhouetted against the evening sky at Exeter. This engine, the only one of the class to be preserved, can now be seen at work on the Severn Valley Railway. 27 March 1965. (*Peter W Gray*)
Agfa Super Silette   Kodachrome II

Above. After nationalisation in 1948 BR wanted to adopt standard liveries for its locomotive fleet. There was an interesting period during 1948 when various experimental colours were tried on different locomotives including LNER apple green with LNWR style lining on a 'Castle'! Eventually it was decreed that the LNWR lined black livery would be used on all mixed traffic classes, and GWR types contained within this definition were so painted. In my view this livery never suited GWR engines at all, although it may have enhanced the appearance of many other railway's locomotives. However, this fine transparency shows in detail 'Hall' No 4903 *Astley Hall* in that livery (although the tender is unlined black) so you may judge for yourself. By 1957 all the GWR mixed traffic classes, and many others, were coming out of former GWR workshops after repairs repainted in Brunswick green with the traditional black and orange lining. Here No 4903 stands in the sunshine at Oxford station working the 2.33 pm Leamington Spa to Paddington. 29 September 1956. (R C Riley)
Agfa Silette f3.5 lens   *Kodachrome 8 ASA f4, 1/60*

Opposite. At Brimscombe, in the Stroud Golden Valley, 'Grange' class No 6863 *Dolhywel Grange* blows off steam, perhaps impatient at being delayed in the up loop line. The up home signal is off to allow oncoming 'Hymek' No D7008 uninterrupted passage with a Cheltenham St James to Paddington train before No 6863 can continue on its journey with the 7.00 am Lydney to High Wycombe ballast train. 26 September 1964. (*Hugh Ballantyne*)
Voigtlander CLR   *Agfa CT18*   *f5.6, 1/250*

Although withdrawal was imminent when this picture was taken, 9400 class No 9493 has steam to spare as she arrives at Downfield Crossing Halt with the 10.20 am from Gloucester Central to Chalford. Five weeks later the 'Chalford Flyer' service ceased and the seven small halts, including this one with its lovely and distinctive 'pagoda' corrugated iron sheeted shelters, were no longer required. It was on this section that the GWR in 1903 inaugurated its system of railcars and halts to serve country areas and small settlements close to the railway. As the halts were cheap to build and the scheme caught on with the public, the idea became successful and was extended over much of the system. 26 September 1964. (*Hugh Ballantyne*)
Voigtlander CLR   Agfa CT18   f8, 1/125

The last design of shunting engine to appear from the GWR in company days was the 9400 class 0–6–0PT introduced by Mr Hawksworth in 1947, when ten were built. Two hundred more were built by contractors between 1949 and 1956 with the bizarre result that some had a working life of only six years. Their tasks were varied, and in the Gloucester area they often worked express London trains on the 7½ mile shuttle service between Gloucester and Cheltenham St James, due to the necessity for all these trains to reverse at Gloucester Central. Here a grubby looking No 9471, built by Robert Stephenson & Hawthorns in 1952, hurries along near Churchdown, correctly displaying 'A class' lamps, with the 3.50 pm Cheltenham to Paddington express. 16 May 1964. (*Hugh Ballantyne*)
Voigtlander CLR   Agfa CT18   f4, 1/500

Above. The majestic sight of a spotless 'King' threading its way out of Paddington past Subway Junction with the 1.55 pm from Paddington to Pembroke Dock and Fishguard as No 6023 *King Edward II* begins to get into his stride for the first stage of the journey of 36 miles before the first stop at Reading. 10 September 1960. *(R C Riley)*
Agfa Super Silette, f2 Solagon lens
Kodachrome 8 ASA   f2, 1/250

Opposite. In the 1950s and 1960s, the Western Region's crack train was the Monday to Friday 'Bristolian', which ran non-stop to and from Paddington on a 105-minute schedule with a limited load of seven vehicles (eight on Monday down and Friday up). In June 1959 the train became diesel-hauled using 'Warships', but on Saturdays, still leaving Paddington at the same time of 8.45 am, it ran with a much heavier load to Weston-super-Mare on a slower schedule which included a stop at Bath. Up until 1962 the

Saturday train also reverted to steam, Old Oak Common indiscriminately providing either a 'King' or 'Castle' Here the Saturday 8.45 am down passes milepost 105 near Bathampton, travelling at speed just before the driver of No 6018 *King Henry VI* applies the brakes for the Bath stop. Note that the 'Bristolian' chocolate and cream stock is included in the train formation. 25 August 1962. *(Hugh Ballantyne)*
Voigtlander CLR   Agfa CT18   f4, 1/250

Opposite. 'Manors' were comparatively rare on the main Bristol–Swindon line so when they appeared their movements were worth recording. On a hot summer Saturday in July the 10.30 am Cardiff to Portsmouth Harbour train produced No 7805 *Broome Manor*, shown slowing down for Bathampton to take the sharp southward curve off the main line before heading down the Limpley Stoke valley of the River Avon out of Somerset into Wiltshire and beyond. 7 July 1962. (*Hugh Ballantyne*)
Voigtlander CLR   Agfa CT18   f5.6, 1/250

Below. The driver of 'Modified Hall' 6959 class No 6994 *Baggrave Hall* is in characteristic pose on the right hand side of the footplate as his engine is panned galloping along the main line towards Bathampton with the 10.50 am Bristol (Temple Meads) to Portsmouth Harbour train. 7 July 1962. (*Hugh Ballantyne*)
Voigtlander CLR   Perutz C18   f8, 1/60

Below. One of the spectacular engineering features of the former Barry Railway was Walnut Tree Viaduct, a massive seven span lattice steel girder structure which soared 120 feet above the River Taff, the quadruple track of the Taff Vale Railway and the main A470 road. This enabled the Barry to bridge the Nantgarw Gap, south of Taffs Well, a narrow defile created from a great natural fault in the rock barrier which marks the southern limit of the Glamorgan coalfield. Here 0–6–2T No 6614 rumbles slowly across with the daily, and then only, train, the 12.30 pm pick-up goods from Aber Junction, Caerphilly. 12 May 1965. (*Hugh Ballantyne*)
Voigtlander CLR   *Agfa CT18*   *f8, 1/125*

Opposite. A bird's eye view looking down from Walnut Tree Viaduct where, 120 feet below on the quadruple track of the former Taff Vale Railway main line, 5600 class 0–6–2T No 5692 is banking a northbound coal train heading towards Nantgarw. 13 May 1965. (*Hugh Ballantyne*)
Voigtlander CLR   *Agfa CT18*   *f11, 1/60*

As a modern supplement to the varied fleet of 0–6–2Ts so popular with the South Wales companies grouped into the GWR by the Railways Act 1921, Mr Collett designed a suitable standard 0–6–2T, the 5600 series. The first appeared in 1924 and two hundred were built, 150 at Swindon and the last batch of 50 by Armstrong Whitworth in 1928. They were competent performers on their territory, equally capable of working heavily laden Welsh valley passenger or coal trains. Here No 5618 is just ex-works, resplendent in lined green livery, and stands in the shed yard at Cardiff Canton. 12 November 1961. (*Hugh Ballantyne*)

Voigtlander CLR   Perutz C18   f5.6, 1/30

Radyr was a neat four road Cardiff valleys shed built in 1931 to replace a former Taff Vale Railway structure on the same site. By the end of 1964 it had an allocation of 43 engines, at that late stage in the Western Region steam era, one of the largest regional shed allocations. Standing outside the shed are two recent transfers from Neath, 0–6–0PTs Nos 9615 and 9656. The shed closed on 26 July 1965 and both engines were withdrawn later in the year. 13 May 1965. (*Hugh Ballantyne*)

Voigtlander CLR   *Agfa CT18*   *f5.6, 1/60*

A former junction station which today bears no resemblance to the view seen here. Once Pontardulais Junction was a substantial station with four platforms where the LNWR line to Swansea Victoria turned south-eastwards away from the GWR line from Llandeilo to Llanelly. Most unusually an 0–6–0PT, No 4674, carrying 'A' class lamps is seen entering the Swansea platform with the 2.40 pm from Shrewsbury to Swansea Victoria. This engine was no doubt a substitute for something considerably larger like an LMS class 5, the type most usually seen on this job, which may have failed en route during the long cross country journey. 19 May 1964. (*Hugh Ballantyne*)

Voigtlander CLR   Agfa CT18   f5.6, 1/250

On a sunny summer morning 5700 class 0–6–0PT No 9669 bathes in the low light amidst the lovely rural surroundings of Bala station, waiting to work the 8.30 am train to Bala Junction. This is only a 3/4 mile journey but it enables passengers from the town to make connection with the long line traversing northern Wales right across the country between Ruabon and Barmouth Junction (now Morfa Mawddach). 29 July 1963. (*Peter A Fry*)
Kodak Retinette IB   Agfa CT18

Above. Light 0–6–0PT No 1661, one of two allocated at Worcester, seen in the shed yard there complete with spark arresting chimney. These engines were employed on shunting duties, including the 'vinegar' branch to the works producing that commodity. The 1600 class, a modernised version of the 2021 class dating back over fifty years previously, did not appear until after the GWR had been nationalised, being built between 1949 and 1955. This particular engine had a life of only nine years from 1955 to 1964. 6 September 1963. (*Hugh Ballantyne*)
Voigtlander CLR   Agfa CT18   f5.6, 1/30

Opposite. No 1363, one of five Churchward-designed 0–6–0STs with outside cylinders for dock shunting, was built at Swindon in 1910. The engine is seen busy at Plymouth pushing a line of oil tank wagons containing diesel loco-motive fuel into position in Laira shed yard. The picture clearly shows the shape of the rear bunker on these engines, quite different in appearance from the usual GWR style of straight back with projecting curved top part of the coal space. No 1363 was withdrawn from service in 1962 and is now preserved by the GWS at Didcot Railway Centre. 30 August 1961. (*R C Riley*)
Agfa Super Silette, f2 Solagon lens
Kodachrome 8 ASA

Opposite. For a time LMS Ivatt-designed class 2 2–6–2Ts were allocated to the Western Region and during the late 1950s and early 1960s some of the type were busy working in the Bristol Division. In this picture No 41208 is coming into Cheddar station with the 2.45 pm Yatton to Witham train. The southern escarpment of the Mendip Hills rises prominently to 500 feet behind the railway, which at this point was about 40 feet above sea level, as the Cheddar Valley branch skirted the range between Axbridge and Wells. 31 August 1963. (*Hugh Ballantyne*)
Voigtlander CLR
Agfa CT18   f5.6, 1/125

Right. In the 1950s the BR Standard designs appeared and brought a new range of distinctive locomotives onto the BR network. There were twelve classes comprising 999 engines of which 188, in four types, were built at Swindon. Over the years the Standards were in service seven types saw regular use on the Western Region. Swindon built all 45 of the class 3 2–6–2T's in the 82000 series between 1951 and 1954, and here, one of the 1953 batch, No 82039, comes into the down platform of Shepton Mallet High Street station with the 3.28 pm train from Witham to Yatton as No 3643 waits to take the 2.45 pm opposite working forward to Witham. 27 July 1963. (*Hugh Ballantyne*)
Voigtlander CLR
Agfa CT18   f8, 1/60

CRANGE COURT JUNCTION

One of the more stylish Standard types was the class 4 2–6–4T, which totalled 155 units, none of which were built at Swindon or originally allocated to the Western Region. However, during the later run down of steam in southern England a few of these big tanks found work on the Western, including No 80100, seen here standing in the branch platform of the weather worn and paint starved but still impressive station at Grange Court Junction, working the 12.15 pm train from Gloucester to Hereford. This locomotive is now preserved on the Bluebell Railway. 26 September 1964. (*Hugh Ballantyne*)
Voigtlander CLR   Agfa CT18   f8, 1/125

The first BR Standard type to appear was the class 7 Pacific and in 1951 the Western found itself host to 15 of the 55 built, the first Pacifics based permanently on the former GWR since the one and only *The Great Bear*. They did good work from Cardiff Canton shed working London–South Wales trains but eventually in 1961 were transferred to the London Midland Region and replaced by 'Castles' and 'Kings'. One of the ex-Western batch, No 70020 *Mer-cury*, found itself back on the territory for a day in 1964, albeit at a most unusual part of it, on the former Midland & South Western Junction Railway. This picture shows No 70020 standing at Ludgershall station having worked down the remnant of this former cross-country railway from Andover Junction with an enthusiasts' special from London. Most of the MSWJR was closed in September 1961, but the southern end remained open for military traffic centred around Tidworth. A feature of the military use can be seen in the extra wide platforms of the station, necessitated by the movement of troops, who when travelling in substantial numbers were paraded on the platform often with large amounts of equipment. 8 March 1964. (*Hugh Ballantyne*)
Voigtlander CLR   Agfa CT18   f8, 1/125

Above. Numerically the largest and most powerful of the Standard engines was the class 9F 2–10–0, of which 251 were built, 43 at Swindon and the remainder at Crewe. They did excellent work on the Western Region and elsewhere, and this picture shows No 92206, built at Swindon in 1957, on the up slow line at milepost 150¼ near Undy, west of Severn Tunnel Junction, with an iron ore empties train. Note the water troughs between the rails of the up and down fast lines and the water tank feeding them on the left. Such features have completely vanished from the railway scene now, but in the steam era were a functional part of railway operated by all four main British railway companies except the Southern Railway. This set of troughs was one of three from which engines working the Paddington to Cardiff run could pick up water. 14 May 1965. (*Hugh Ballantyne*)
Voigtlander CLR   Agfa CT18   f5.6, 1/250

Opposite. Heading westwards on the down relief line towards Undy and Newport, with part of Severn Tunnel Junction's marshalling yard visible behind, is class 9F No 92250 with a goods train. Built in December 1958, not only was this the highest numbered engine in the BR fleet, but it was also the only BR Standard engine to be fitted with a Giesl ejector. This experimental modification was carried out in 1959 and although the ejector was not adopted for further use by BR this particular locomotive retained the system until it was withdrawn. The long narrow chimney of the ejector can be clearly seen in this picture. 11 May 1965. (*Hugh Ballantyne*)
Voigtlander CLR   Agfa CT18   f5.6, 1/250

A unique event was enterprisingly organised by the photographer when 0–4–2T No 1458 was sent out from Oswestry Works on a test run to Welshpool. This coincided with the Welshpool & Llanfair Railway Preservation Society, which had by this time taken over the W & L narrow gauge line from BR, placing ex-GWR No 822 *The Earl* in the narrow gauge yard at Welshpool. The standard gauge 1400 class 0–4–2T was then carefully brought into the little used market siding and placed conveniently alongside. The result is this rare transparency, enabling us to make a direct comparison of size and scale between a small standard gauge engine and the little Beyer Peacock-built 2 ft 6 in gauge 0–6–0T beside it. 16 July 1963. (*Basil Roberts*) *Kodak Retinette IB   Agfa CT18*

At one time the 1 ft 11½ in gauge Vale of Rheidol section of the GWR left Aberystwyth from lines placed just outside the southern wall of the standard gauge station. Where these trains stand now forms part of a car park as the narrow gauge tracks have been moved into the station, their ground level platforms situated on the trackbed of the former Carmarthen lines. On a showery 1960 August Bank Holiday the old station presents a busy scene as No 7 *Owain Glyndŵr* is about to leave with the 1.45 pm to Devil's Bridge, to be followed at 2.30 pm by No 9 *Prince of Wales*. 1 August 1960. (*Michael Mensing*)

Voigtlander Bessa II   Agfa CT18   f9, 1/50

Despite the delapidated condition of the shed building and grime covered locomotives, the preparation of two 'Castles' in the early morning sunlight still proved a stirring sight. Nos 7001 *Sir James Milne* and 5026 *Criccieth Castle* are seen in this picture raising steam at Wolverhampton Stafford Road shed and getting ready to work Saturday holiday trains to the south west of England. 24 August 1963. (*Hugh Ballantyne*) *Voigtlander CLR*   *Agfa CT18*

This picture sadly portrays just how the Western Region steam fleet was allowed to deteriorate during the last year or so until final elimination in December 1965. Once gleaming 'Modified Halls' now neglected, dirty and devoid of their name and numberplates stand in the shed yard at Oxford waiting their next spell of duty. Nearest the camera is No 6967 ex-*Willesley Hall* on its home patch with No 6983 ex-*Otterington Hall* from Didcot behind. On the right is the tender of Standard class 5 No 75021 from Gloucester and then home-based 2–6–2T No 6108. By the end of 1964 Oxford's allocation was down to 27 engines, ten of them 'Halls'. No 6967 survived until December 1965 but No 6983 was withdrawn in the month the photograph was taken. 15 August 1965. (*Hugh Ballantyne*)
Voigtlander CLR   Agfa CT18   f5.6, 1/60

Bristol Temple Meads during the transition from steam to diesel traction in the early 1960s is epitomised here by the unkempt appearance of the 'Castle' drawing out of this impressive station with a Whit Monday excursion from Birmingham Snow Hill to Weston-super-Mare. Looking on in the background are three of the Western Region's then modern fleet of diesel-hydraulic 'Hymeks'. They, like No 7024 *Powis Castle* in the foreground, have all long been withdrawn. 3 June 1963. (*Hugh Ballantyne*)
Voigtlander CLR   Agfa CT18   f8, 1/125

Opposite. A sad sight indeed but it was a fact that steam on the Western Region became, and looked, very run down by 1964. A once shining No 7019 *Fowey Castle*, reduced to a grimy state, is in keeping with its menial task of hauling an up unfitted goods train past Grange Court Junction en route from Severn Tunnel Junction to Gloucester. Behind the train lies part of the Forest of Dean and curving away to the right is the line to Ross-on-Wye and Hereford. 26 September 1964. (*Hugh Ballantyne*)
Voigtlander CLR   Agfa CT18   f5.6, 1/250

In 1957, to the pleasure of the thousands of GWR enthusiasts, *City of Truro*, which had stood since 1931 as a silent Great Western outcast amongst mainly LNER constituent company locomotives on display in the old York Railway Museum, was restored to operating condition by Swindon Works and came back into service that year. Not surprisingly she was in demand for specials, but between such work was given regular jobs on local trains in the Swindon and Didcot area. In this picture the classic lines of the GWR outside framed 4–4–0 are well portrayed as this lovely engine approaches Appleford Crossing, north of Didcot, with an SLS enthusiasts' special returning to Birmingham Snow Hill. 16 June 1957. (*R C Riley*)
Agfa Silette, f2 Solagon lens
Kodachrome 8 ASA
f2, 1/250